Rainbow the Cat
Goes to the Farm

Author: Anna Banas-chen
Illustrator: Julia wu/Lillian Lin

This book teaches kids about farm animals.
Come along with Rainbow the Cat to learn fun
facts about animals found on the farm.

This book has been translated into Chinese, French and Spanish.

Acknowledgments

This book is dedicated to my grandparents Bob and Agnes, Mingshou, and my parents Mike and Emma. Thank you for your love and support for my second book! Nai Nai Yimei Ye (Judy), I miss you.

Special thanks to my teacher Mrs. Janice Currie for teaching me everything, and my horseback riding instructor Heather Reynolds for teaching me about horses.

One day after school, Rainbow the Cat went with her mom to the farm. She was excited. She wanted to learn how to ride horses. Rainbow the Cat did not realize how many other animals can be found on the farm. Do you know what animals you can see at a farm?

When she got there, she saw some sheep eating grass, some chickens chasing each other and ducks in the pond.

Rainbow met Heather, her horseback
riding instructor.

Heather showed Rainbow the Cat her horse named Lemon. Rainbow took her first lesson in horseback riding. Soon, her lesson was over, but she still had to brush Lemon and feed her dinner. Rainbow put the food in her stall, and the water in Lemon's bucket.

Fun facts about horses:
- Baby horses are called foals. Foals can run shortly after being born.
- Horses can sleep lying down and standing up.
- Horses can run up to 45 miles per hour.
- Horses are large, strong and smart.

What do horses eat and how do people feed them?
Horses eat hay, grass and grains at mealtime. You can give them fruits and vegetables as snacks. Horses need a lot of water to drink.

Next, Rainbow the Cat was going to see the chickens. They had white and brown feathers. Angelo was the name of the rooster.

<u>Fun facts about chickens and roosters:</u>
- A young chicken is called a chick.
- Chickens live in a chicken coop.
- An adult male chicken is called a "rooster". An adult female is called a "hen".
- Hens lay eggs which hatch into chicks.
- Roosters can crow.

<u>What do chickens eat and how do people feed them?</u>
Chickens like to scratch and peck at the ground for bugs. Chickens also eat grains, and vegetables. Chickens drink water from a water dish in their chicken coop. Do not use your hand to feed them because they can bite you.

Rainbow the Cat walked over to see the sheep. They were fuzzy and cute! Rainbow saw a baby sheep. His name was Oscar, he loved to frolic and jump!

<u>Fun facts about sheep:</u>
- Young sheep are called lambs.
- Female sheep are called ewes. Adult male sheep are known as rams.
- Sheep live in a large group called a flock.
- Sheep have a thick coat called wool, it can be used to make clothing and blankets.

<u>What do sheep eat and how do people feed them?</u>
Sheep eat grass from pastures. When you feed sheep, you put your hands flat, and hold the food on your palm, and they will use their tongue to eat it.

Rainbow looked in the next pasture, there was a bull named Bob.

<u>Fun facts about cows:</u>
- Baby cows are called calves.
- Cows cannot see the colors red and green.
- Cows have good hearing.
- Everyday a cow can spend 8 hours eating, 8 hours chewing and 8 hours sleeping.

<u>What do cows eat and how do people feed them?</u>
Baby calves drink milk. Cows eat grains mixed with hay, corn silage (entire corn plant chopped and fermented). People put the food in the cow barn or put the food in the feeding bucket. Cows also love to eat grass.

Rainbow went to check out the pig pen.
Emma the pig rolled around in the mud.

<u>Fun facts about pigs:</u>
- Pigs are intelligent animals.
- Pigs are omnivores, meaning they eat both plants and other animals.
- Pigs have an excellent sense of smell.
- Some people like to keep pigs as pets.
- Wild pigs are called boar.

<u>What do pigs eat and how do people feed them?</u>
Pigs eat grains, fruits and vegetables. Do not feed pigs with your hand, they can bite!

Rainbow explored a wooden hutch. That is where the bunny Agnes lived.

<u>Fun facts about bunnies:</u>
- Bunnies are born with their eyes closed and without fur.
- A young rabbit is called a kit.
- A female rabbit is called a doe.
- A male rabbit is called a buck.
- Rabbits are herbivores, they only eat plants.
- Rabbit's teeth never stop growing!
- A rabbit can make a great pet.

<u>What do rabbits eat and how do people feed them?</u>
Plants and vegetables. Especially carrots! People can put the food on the ground, or in a bowl and they will eat it.

Rainbow saw a goose named Mike, running around.

Fun facts about geese:
- Geese migrate every year.
- Geese can live almost anywhere.
- Geese fly in a "V" shape.
- Geese are related to Ducks and Swans.
- DO NOT play with geese, they can chase and bite you!

What do geese eat and how do people feed them?
Geese eat seeds, nuts, grass, plants and berries. People can feed them by spreading food out in the grass, or in a large bowl.

Nearby, Kiki the kitten napped in the sun.

<u>Fun facts about kittens:</u>
- Kittens are blind and deaf until 2 to 3 weeks old.
They need their mom during this time.
- All kittens are born with blue eyes.
- Kittens have a strong sense of smell.
- Kittens have 26 teeth.

<u>What do kittens eat and how do people feed them?</u>
- Kittens can't drink cow milk. It will upset their stomach.
They can drink special kitten formula if needed.
- Kittens can eat wet or dry kitten food, or
home-made food out of a bowl.
- Kittens love fish.

Next, Rainbow saw a big bird, it was a turkey.
Her name was Amy.

<u>Fun facts about turkeys:</u>
- A group of turkeys is called a flock.
- Turkeys have 2 stomachs.
- Male turkeys have loose skin by their beak called a waddle.

<u>What do turkeys eat and how do people feed them?</u>
Turkeys are herbivores. They like to eat the growing tips of the grass.
They also enjoy lettuce, tomatoes, sweet corn and summer squash.

Rainbow heard a sound coming from the barn. "Hee-haw!"
What animal makes that sound? It was Leo, a donkey foal.

<u>Fun facts about donkeys:</u>
- Donkeys are related to horses and zebras.
- A boy donkey is called a jack.
- A girl donkey is called a jenny.
- Donkeys can be stubborn.

<u>What do donkeys eat and how do people feed them?</u>
Donkeys eat hay and grass from the pasture.
You can feed them hay and grains in the barn, too.

Quack! Quack! Rainbow saw Ben the duck swimming in the pond with his friends.

Fun facts about ducks:
- A baby duck is called a duckling.
- Ducks are water birds, like geese and swans.
- Ducks' feathers are waterproof.
- Very few ducks actually "quack", however, they can make a lot of other sounds.

What do ducks eat and how do people feed them?
Ducks eat grass, aquatic plants, insects, seeds, fruit, fish, vegetables and grains. You can throw the food to them in the pond or on the grass.

In the pasture, there was a baby goat named Lydia. Rainbow stood on the fence to say hello.

<u>Fun facts about goats:</u>
- Young goats are called kids.
- Goat kids learn to stand right after they are born.
- Kids begin climbing and jumping when they are a week old.
- Goat kids like to snuggle, just like human kids.
- Goat kids make sounds that are called a bleat. Mother and kid goats recognize each other's bleats.

<u>What do goats eat and how do people feed them?</u>
Goats are known for eating everything! Even cardboard, tin cans and clothing.(But that isn't healthy for them!)- Goats like to eat plants, leaves, bushes, grass and hay. If you want to feed them grains, you can hold your hand flat, they will lick it off your hand.

Rainbow heard some noise nearby; puppies were wrestling in the grass! Rainbow watched Sancho the puppy play.

<u>Fun facts about puppies:</u>
- Puppies spend 15 to 20 hours a day sleeping.
- Puppies become 'adults' when they turn one year old.
- Puppies are born without teeth.
- Newborn puppies can't poop.
- Puppies can be twins. Double the cuteness.

<u>What do puppies eat and how do people feed them?</u>
- Puppies drink their mother's milk till 4 weeks old, and then they start eating dog food.
- You can put the food in their bowl.
- They drink water or special puppies' formula milk.

Zac, a llama came by to see Rainbow.

<u>Fun facts about llamas:</u>
- Llamas are related to camels.
- Llamas help people carry heavy loads.
- People use their wool to make fabric for clothing.

<u>What do llamas eat and how do people feed them?</u>
Llamas are herbivores, they only eat plants. Hold your hand flat and they will eat the food from your hand.

There was a pony on the farm. Her name was Astrid.
Rainbow meowed hello to Astrid.

<u>Fun facts about ponies:</u>
- Ponies are small horses.
- Young ponies are called foals.
- Shetland ponies are small but strong.
- Well-trained ponies are good for children to learn to ride.

<u>What do ponies eat and how to feed them?</u>
- Ponies mostly eat hay and grass.
- Sometimes they eat grains such as, corn or oats.
- You can put their food in their bucket.

"Hiss!" Rainbow the cat heard something in the pasture where the sheep were eating. It was a "rainbow" snake! Rainbow was afraid until she remembered her mom said not to be afraid of snakes. Rainbow was thinking, for this rainbow snake, Anna was a good name. Snakes are not farm animals, but you can find snakes in pastures and in nearby woods.

<u>Fun facts about snakes:</u>
- Snakes can swallow their food, called prey, whole.
- Snakes shed their skin as they grow bigger.
- Snakes can be venomous or non-venomous, it is best to leave them alone.
- Snakes are carnivores, or meat eaters, just like Rainbow the Cat.
- Snakes are not slimy! Their scales are smooth and help them slither.

Now it was time to leave, Rainbow the Cat had a great time. She loves the farm and she cannot wait to come back to visit again.

Lilin·Julia·Wu is the little painter of this book. She is an 8 year old third grader living in Shenzhen, China. Julia is very talented and she loves arts and making handcrafts. Since she was younger, she has traveled around the world and become familiar with different cultures and arts. She is an animal lover. Julia is looking forward to have more opportunities to discover animals and the world. She has the ambition to be educated in the greatest arts university.

Xueying Lin, the co-illustrator of this book graduated from University of the Arts London.

The profit from this book will be donated to:

(1) **United Nations The Food and Agriculture Organization (FAO)** - United Nations The Food and Agriculture Organization is a specialized agency of the United Nations that leads international efforts to defeat hunger. FAO's goal is to achieve food security for all and make sure that people have regular access to enough high-quality food to lead active, healthy lives. With over 194 member states, FAO works in over 130 countries worldwide. We believe that everyone can play a part in ending hunger. Join us in creating a #ZeroHunger world.

(2) **The Zoo in Forest Park & Education Center** is a 127-year-old nonprofit organization in Springfield, Mass., dedicated to wildlife education, conservation and rehabilitation. The Zoo in Forest Park is home to more than 225 exotic and native species, the majority of which have been deemed non-releasable due to injury, illness, permanent disability or other factors.

(3) **Pony Club** - The United States Pony Clubs, Inc. started in 1954 to teach riding and the proper care of horses. It is based on The British Pony Club, which was created in 1929 as a junior branch of the Institute of the Horse. Since then, Pony Club has expanded to many countries around the world, with the main goal being to promote sportsmanship, stewardship and leadership through horsemanship.

Book reviews:

"*Anna Banas-Chen does it again! Another remarkable book by a remarkable young lady. Rainbow the Cat is back, and this time goes to the farm to explore and introduce children of all ages to these special animals. Not only does Rainbow the Cat meet farm animals, but the fun facts add even more learning to this experience. Angelo the rooster makes his debut, and all the animals really come to life as Rainbow the Cat visits them. I can't wait to see where Rainbow the Cat and Anna take us next.*" **- State Representative Angelo J. Puppolo, Jr.   Chairman, House Committee on Technology and Intergovernmental Affairs**

"*Another delightful and engaging hit from Anna Banas-Chen with Rainbow the Cat: Goes to the Farm. One of my favorite elements is the "fun facts" section for each animal. As an example, I learned that pigs have an excellent sense of smell. The combination of Anna's prose and Julia Wu's delightful illustrations immediately drew my interest, despite being long past childhood. This is the essence of Anna's appeal - her stories resonate on a multi-generational, multicultural level. In times of challenge and stress, Anna's fresh look at the world revitalizes and educates. I eagerly await the next book in the series and am thrilled to share Anna's work with everyone I know*" **– Kristina Hallett, PhD, Keynote Speaker, TEDx Speaker, Author, Clinical Psychologist, Associate Professor**

"*Anna's second book following Rainbow the Cat's visit to the farm reaches into every fun and interesting nook of a working farm. Rainbow's tour of the whole farm teaches readers about so many different animals-- from geese to pigs to bunnies to cows, and many more! Readers will enjoy Rainbow's new adventure as well as soak up the snapshots chock-full of information. These are pages which will surely require many readings to learn all there is to know about the animals. In this great book, story telling and learning go paw-in-hoof!*" **– Julia Gooding, Ed.M., Harvard Graduate School of Education, International Educator**

"*Wow, what an amazing trip for Rainbow the Cat goes to the farm. Reading this book with kids, knowing and enjoying the life of those farm animals, will surely make us smile, feel peace and love. During a hard time like this, is this what we need to remind of every family, parents and kids: what a wonderful world this is?! I can't wait for the next journey with Rainbow the Cat, and I am sure that is going to be another experience full of imagination.*" **– Haian Lin, Attorney, Adjunct Professor**

"*In her second book, Anna leads readers through an adventure on the farm. I enjoyed reading about all the variety of friends that Rainbow the Cat encounters, as well as the interesting facts included about each new animal! Anna's own curiosity and desire to share her passion for animals is clear in her writing, an exciting synthesis of exploration and knowledge within Rainbow the Cat's story. I look forward to seeing where Anna takes Rainbow the Cat next!*" **– Mina Liang, Distinguished Young Woman of Massachusetts**

Made in the USA
Middletown, DE
06 August 2023

36236663R00029